Origami

A Step by Step Guide

Robert Harbin

Hamlyn

LONDON · NEW YORK · SYDNEY · TORONTO

My grateful thanks to all those folders who have contributed models for this book, and especially Patricia Crawford of America, who has allowed me to illustrate so many of her remarkable creations.

Published by
The Hamlyn Publishing Group Ltd
London · New York · Sydney · Toronto
Astronaut House, Feltham, Middlesex, England

© Copyright Robert Harbin 1974

Printed in England by Chapel River Press, Andover, Hampshire

ISBN 0 600 38109 9

Contents

Introduction

Origami is a Japanese word which means paper-folding. For many hundreds of years the Japanese have cultivated this art-form.

In the last seventeen years origami has become a sophisticated Western pastime, and countless new models have been created in America, Great Britain, the Continent and the Latin countries.

All you need is a piece of foldable paper and an idea in mind, and sooner or later something delightful will evolve.

Origami – A Step By Step Guide leads you gently into this old and very exciting world. If you manage to make every model described in this book you will indeed be a folding convert – one of the dedicated.

If origami is something new for you it is essential that you begin at the beginning. On no account must you try the difficult folds before you have completed some of the more simple models, and begun to understand what the hobby is all about.

This book features a collection of remarkable folds by Patricia Crawford of America. Her folds are very complicated and in some cases quite difficult to do . . . but be assured you can, with a little concentration, get just as good a result as the creator herself.

Origami is not meant to be easy. Origami is a challenge and it is possible that some time will pass before you solve all the problems I have laid before you.

If you are already a keen paper-folder, then you will be very excited when you find just how many new and wonderful folds there are in these pages, and I am sure that the fine colour reproductions of the finished models will give you added incentive.

Although I have tried to put as much detail as possible into the illustrations, and provide as many step by step drawings as possible, a great deal is left for you to discover from the signs, symbols, and a few helpful words.

Symbols

The symbols are based on Akira Yoshizawa's code of lines and arrows. The first thing to do is to study and remember the symbols. Once you get these signs and symbols well into your head, following the step by step illustrations will be no problem for you.

Each drawing really tells its story. Examine the symbols carefully, and immediately you should know what to do. However, in many cases a few words of explanation have been inserted here and there. These should not be necessary, but may help a beginner.

The symbols are self-explanatory. The little arrows tell you just what to do. One arrow means fold in front, another fold behind, and yet another fold under or into and so on.

Most books on origami adopt a set of symbols very like the ones in this book, and if there are differences you will soon see just what they are.

The first few pages contain several simple folds which will give you as much practice as you need to tackle the more advanced folds.

Try to read the symbols and *see* in your mind just how a fold must be made.

So . . . for ten minutes, study those symbols . . .

Pre-Creasing

This means that in order to make the model easier to fold, a certain amount of preliminary creasing is necessary. Once these essential creases have been made it is then comparatively simple to arrive at the correct result.

Patricia Crawford's 'Bird Bath' is a typical example of detailed pre-creasing. Once the creases have been made the rest of the folds are fairly simple.

When pre-creasing, it is necessary to find some guide lines and wherever possible these have been given, so that when the first few folds are made other guide lines are automatically created, and so on until all the folds have been made.

Procedures

In origami there are several standard procedures which you may or may not already know. In the early pages you will notice that certain procedures are shown in detail. For example: on page 12 you will see in Figs. 1 to 10 that flaps are lifted and pressed flat – they are 'squashed.' This will happen a number of times.

On page 11 you will see how to 'sink' two corners, Figs. 24, 25 and 26: how first of all you pre-crease, then stretch out and 'push in.' This will happen again several times but not always in the same way: see page 75, Figs. 6, 7, 8 and 9 and so on.

The 'Petal-fold' is always being used: see page 10, Figs. 10 to 19. Petal-folds need not always be exactly this shape but the procedure is always the same.

If you come across a written instruction to do this or that or the other and you don't know just what is meant, take a look through the index and see where an example of this fold occurs.

'Reverse-folds' will play a big part in your life. 'The Guillemot' is a working example of a series of reverse-folds: inside reverse-folds and outside reverse-folds. In this case pre-creasing helps as you will clearly see.

As you work your way through this and other origami books you will become familiar with 'procedures', and after a while they will become second nature.

Bases

There are many bases: traditional bases and bases created by folders. The Preliminary Base, page 9, the Water-Bomb Base, page 13, the Bird Base, page 10, are a few of the many you will come into contact with.

Most creative folders have bases from which they make many folds. Men like Neal Elias and Fred Rohm of the USA are examples of this. Mr Fred Rohm has what he calls his Simplex Base, from which countless folds have been made, especially working models.

In this book you will notice that the 'Mermaid,' 'Christ on the Mount of Olives,' and the 'Squirrel on the Log' all begin in much the same way.

The Bird Base, the most famous of all traditional bases, has been most used. Then there is the Stretched Bird Base, the Blintzed Bird Base, and so on. Sometimes two bases are mixed together; you will begin to recognise them and probably invent a couple of your own.

Once you are familiar with some of these beginnings you will be able to create your own models. The most popular first creations are, some sort of bird, a decorative design, or a box – and then, who knows? something bigger and better.

So watch out for, and become familiar with, the Bases.

Paper

Almost any paper will do, but fine papers make fine models. Do not just tear a piece of paper out of an exercise book and expect to make a neat and attractive model.

If you need a square it must be exactly square; if a triangle or a rectangle the measurements must be exact, otherwise the resulting model will be a monstrosity.

Papers specially made for origami can be found in many shops, and all attractive wrapping papers cut to size are ideal. You will notice that Patricia Crawford uses foils. These metallic papers keep good shape and are in some cases essential for the models described.

Contacts

GREAT BRITAIN:
The Secretary,
British Origami Society,
193, Abbey Road,
Smethwick, Warley, Staffs.

AMERICA:
The Origami Centre,
71, West Eleventh St.,
New York 2,
NY, USA.

THE SYMBOLS – These should be memorised now

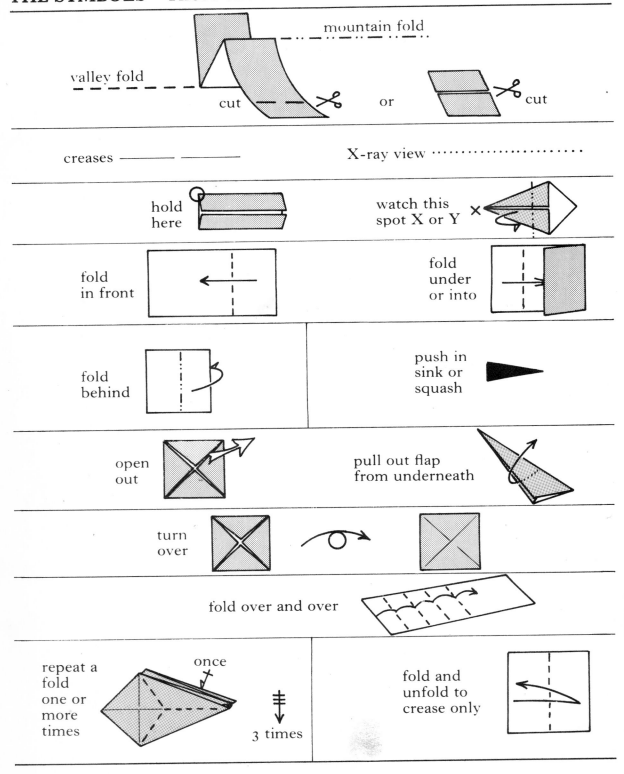

mountain fold

valley fold

cut   or   cut

creases ———   X-ray view ·················

hold here

watch this spot X or Y

fold in front

fold under or into

fold behind

push in sink or squash

open out

pull out flap from underneath

turn over

fold over and over

repeat a fold one or more times   once

3 times

fold and unfold to crease only

HOW TO USE THE SYMBOLS Making a flower

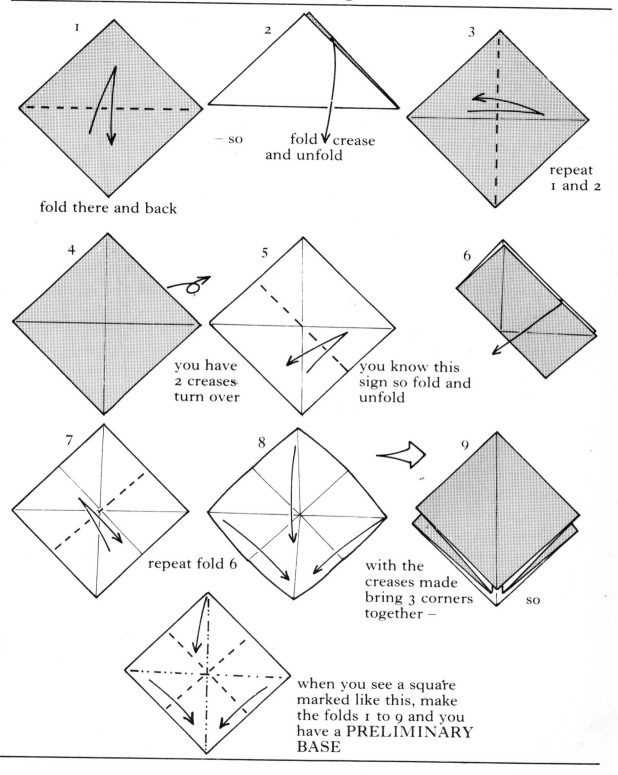

1 fold there and back

2 — so fold crease and unfold

3 repeat 1 and 2

4 you have 2 creases turn over

5 you know this sign so fold and unfold

6

7 repeat fold 6

8 with the creases made bring 3 corners together —

9 so

when you see a square marked like this, make the folds 1 to 9 and you have a PRELIMINARY BASE

USE OF SYMBOLS Making a flower *(continued)*

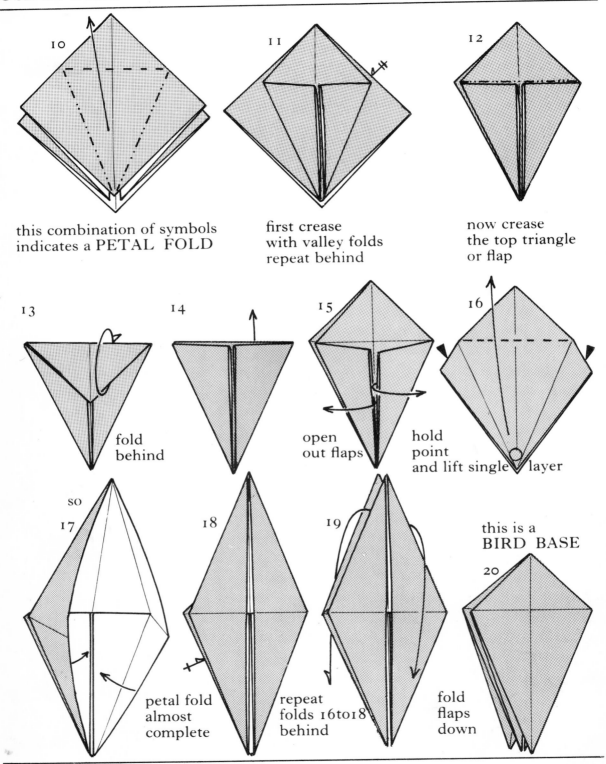

10 this combination of symbols indicates a PETAL FOLD

11 first crease with valley folds repeat behind

12 now crease the top triangle or flap

13 fold behind

14

15 open out flaps hold point and lift single layer

16

so 17

18 petal fold almost complete

19 repeat folds 16 to 18 behind

20 this is a BIRD BASE fold flaps down

Making a flower Philip Shen Hong Kong

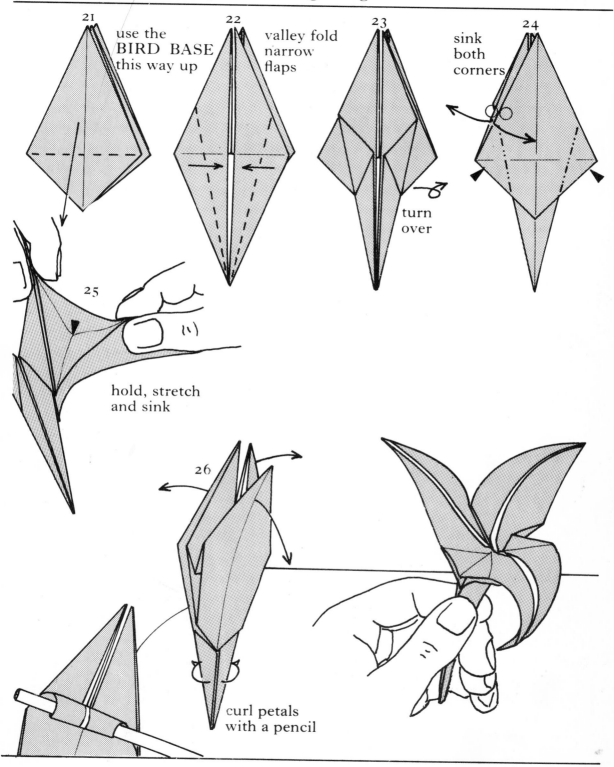

21 use the BIRD BASE this way up

22 valley fold narrow flaps

23 turn over

24 sink both corners

25 hold, stretch and sink

26 curl petals with a pencil

USE OF SYMBOLS Japanese Box

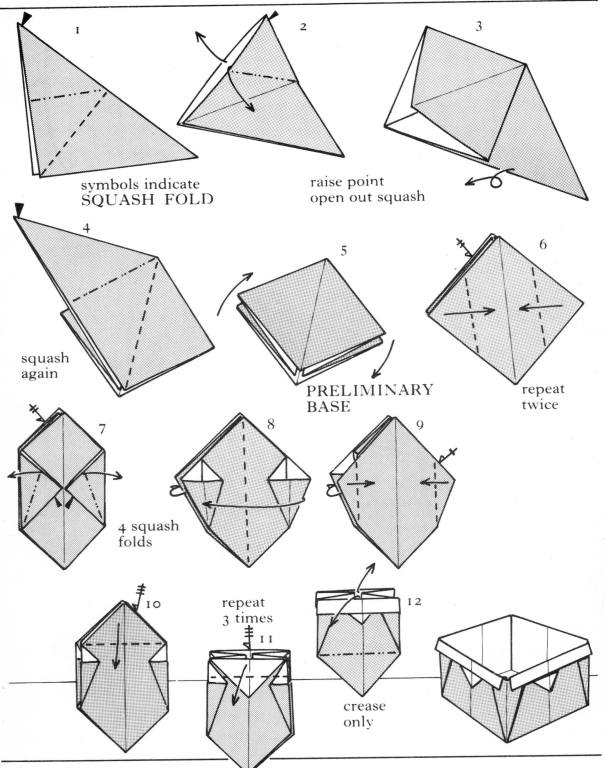

1

symbols indicate
SQUASH FOLD

2

raise point
open out squash

3

4

squash
again

5

PRELIMINARY
BASE

6

repeat
twice

7

4 squash
folds

8

9

10

repeat
3 times

11

12

crease
only

USE OF SYMBOLS Waterbomb Base

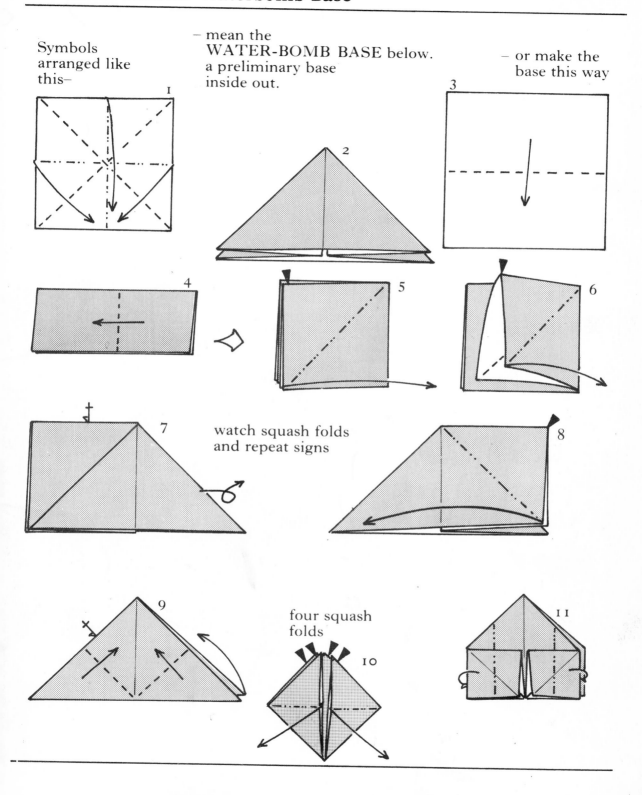

Symbols arranged like this–

– mean the WATER-BOMB BASE below. a preliminary base inside out.

– or make the base this way

watch squash folds and repeat signs

four squash folds

USE OF SYMBOLS Church and Fancy Box

The water-bomb base is the starting point for
endless models. Here are two.

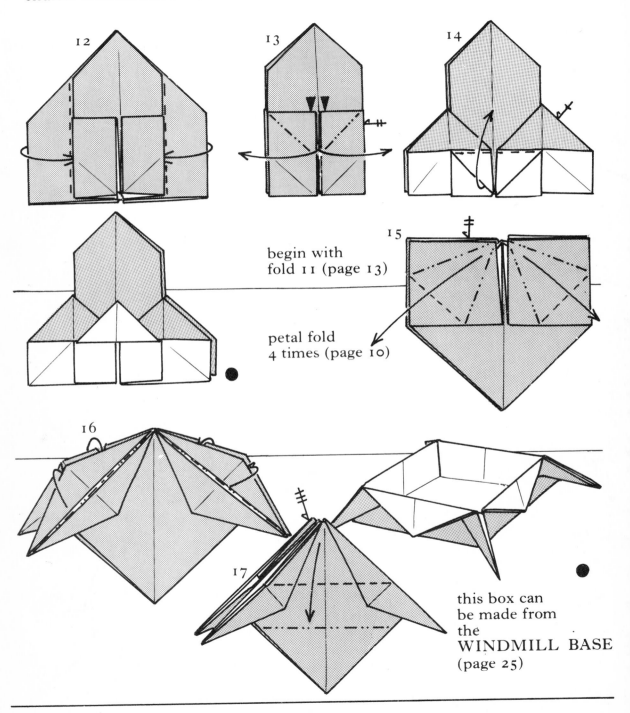

begin with
fold 11 (page 13)

petal fold
4 times (page 10)

this box can
be made from
the
WINDMILL BASE
(page 25)

Lover's Knot – Traditional *An exercise*

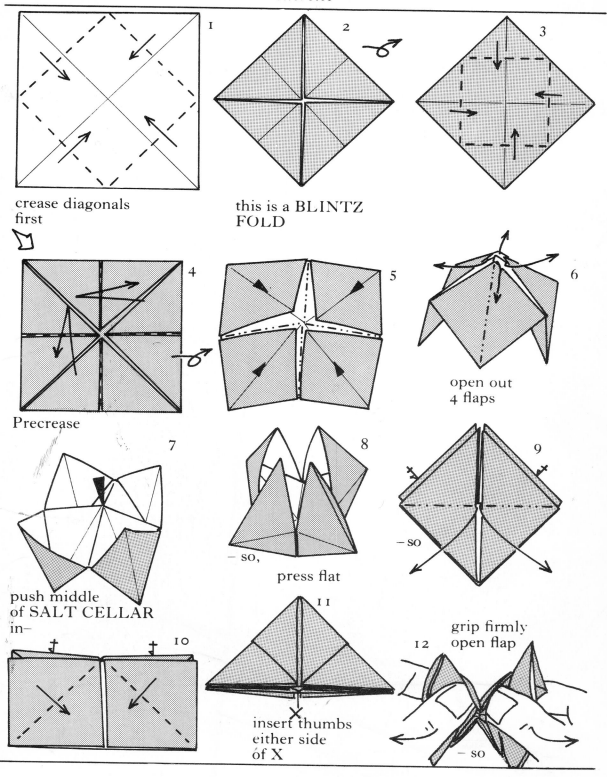

crease diagonals
first

this is a BLINTZ
FOLD

Precrease

open out
4 flaps

push middle
of SALT CELLAR
in–

– so,

press flat

– so

insert thumbs
either side
of X

grip firmly
open flap

– so

Lover's Knot (*continued*)

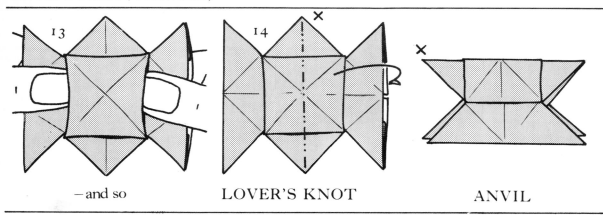

—and so   LOVER'S KNOT   ANVIL

Super-Box John Richardson Gt. Britain

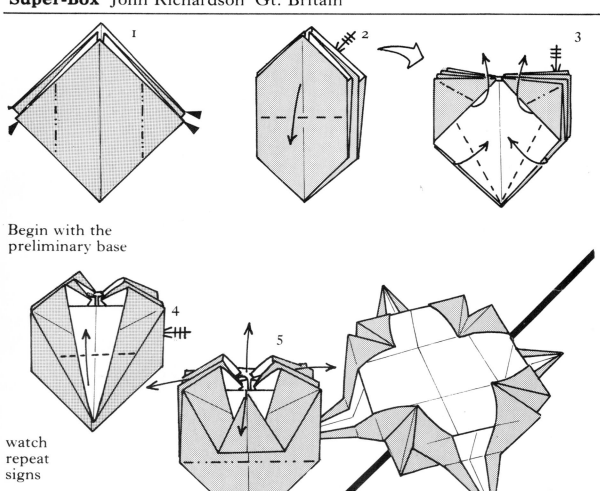

Begin with the
preliminary base

watch
repeat
signs

Guillemot Robert Harbin Gt. Britain

Use a square
black on one side.
Follow the symbols.

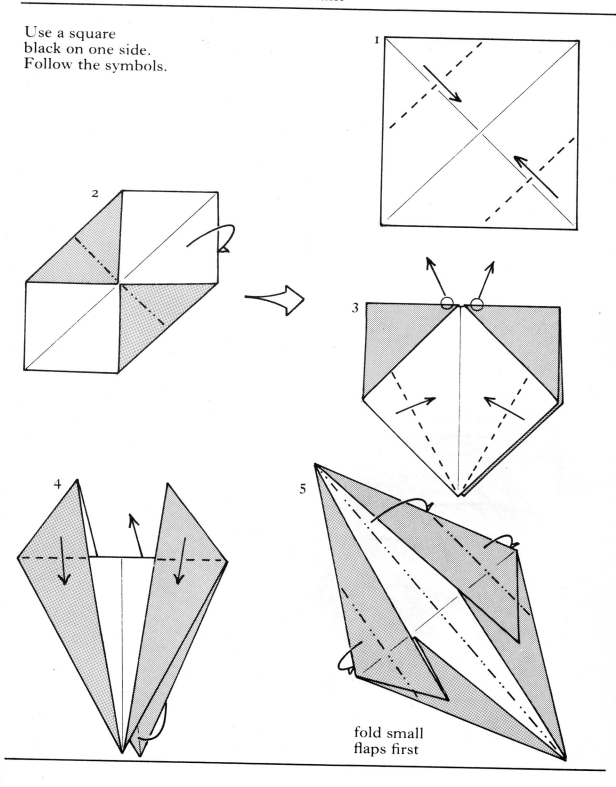

fold small
flaps first

(Above) *Japanese box, Octahedron*
(Opposite) *Paper flowers*

Guillemot (continued)

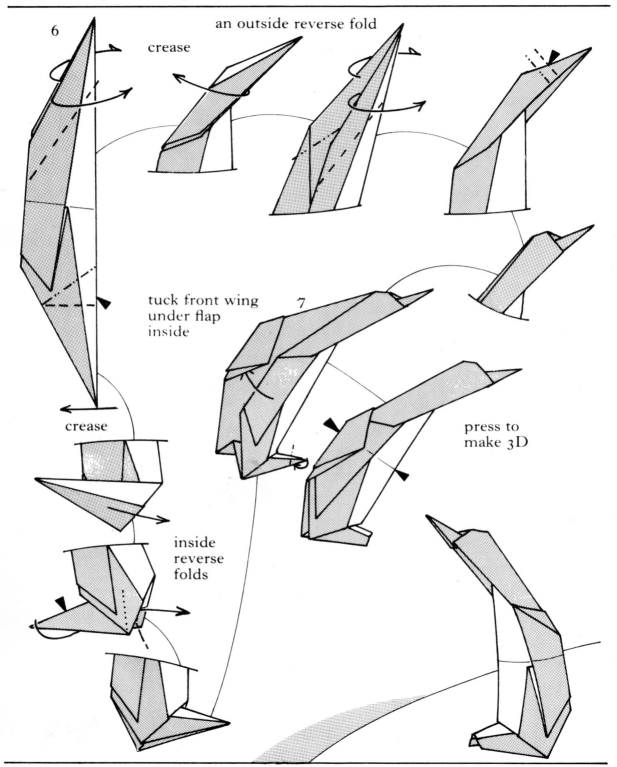

6

crease

an outside reverse fold

tuck front wing
under flap
inside

7

press to
make 3D

crease

inside
reverse
folds

Tetrahedron (Geometric solid) Patricia Crawford America

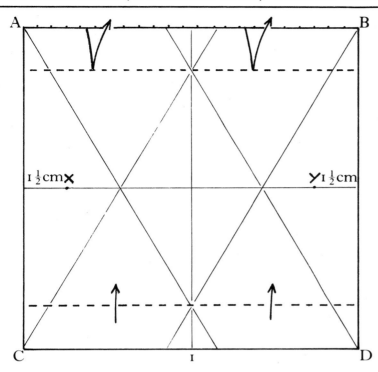

Use a square, $(11\frac{1}{2}$cm)
Make middle creases

Fold corners A and C
to Y make creases

Fold corners B and D
to X make creases
Crease top flap
fold bottom flap

crease as
indicated
and then
fold left

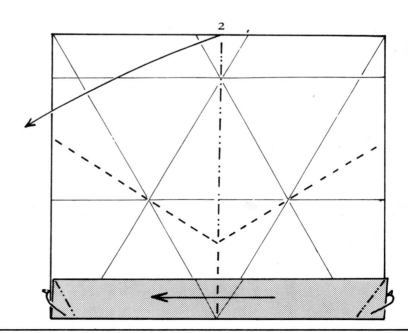

small flaps
folded behind

(Above) Lover's Knot, Super box
(Opposite) Waterbomb base, Church, Fancy box

Tetrahedron *(continued)*

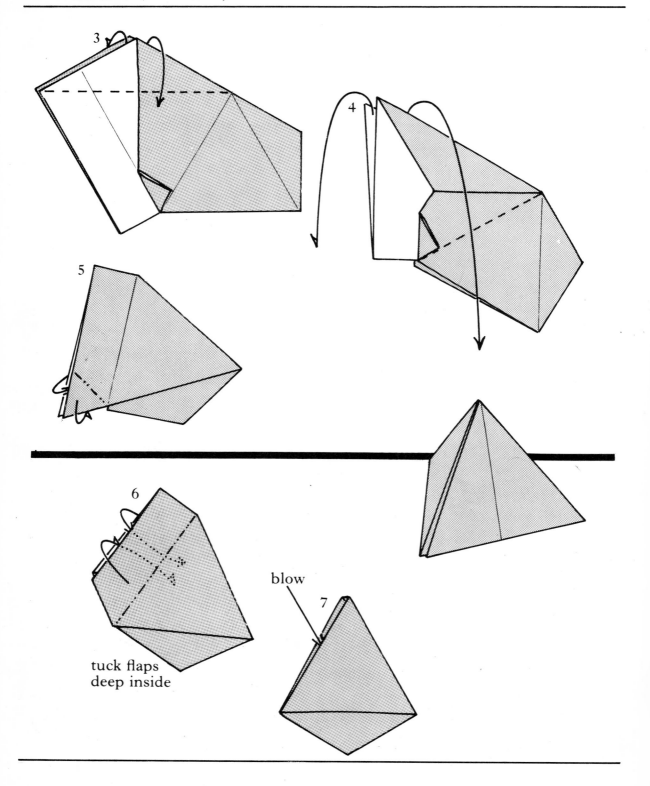

3

4

5

6

blow

7

tuck flaps
deep inside

Decoration Folding exercise Japan

Use a square, either side up. Creases 1 to 5 produce 7.
Squash folds produce 8, the Windmill Base. With this base
endless decorative folds can be devised. 8 squash folds are used fig. 10.

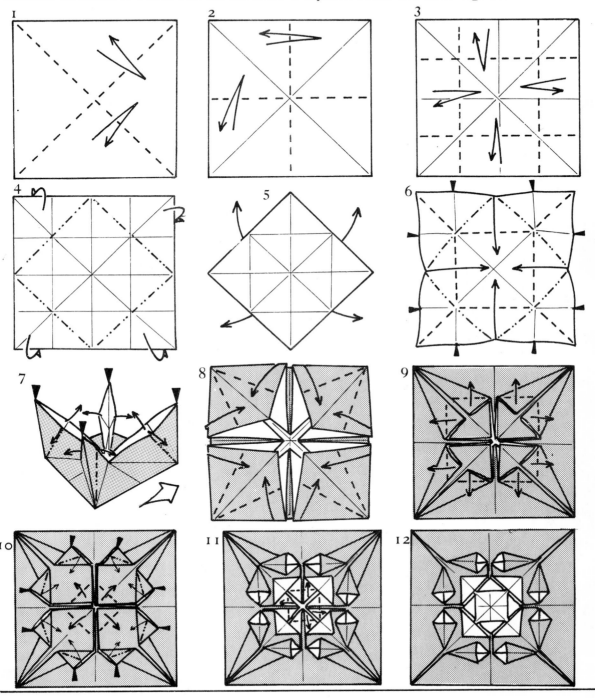

Guillemots

Tetrahedron, Simple dart and Japanese folding exercise

Yacht Toshi Takahama Japan

An example of this lady's genius.
Five simple folds make a yacht.

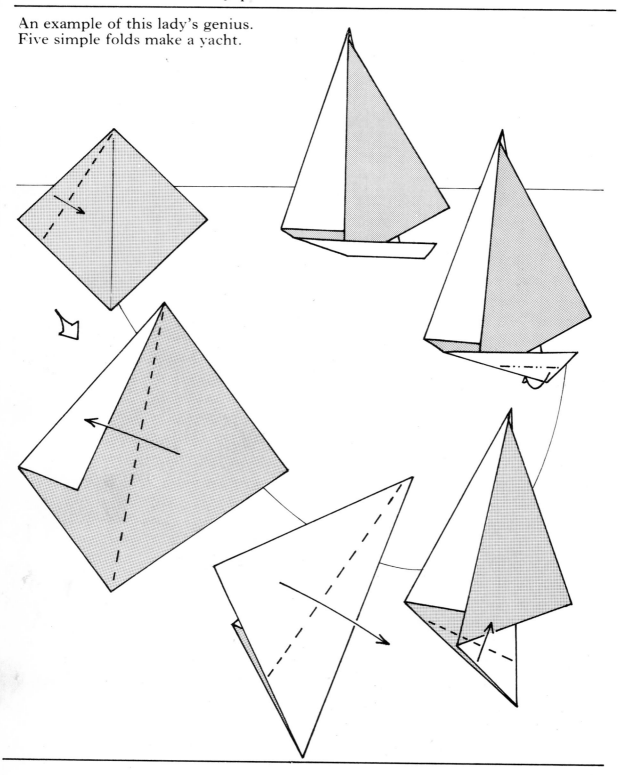

Speedboat Ian Archer *(age 13)* Gt. Britain

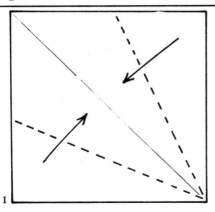

For this outboard motor craft, crease a square along diagonal and fold in sides.

In 5 crease the long narrow flaps

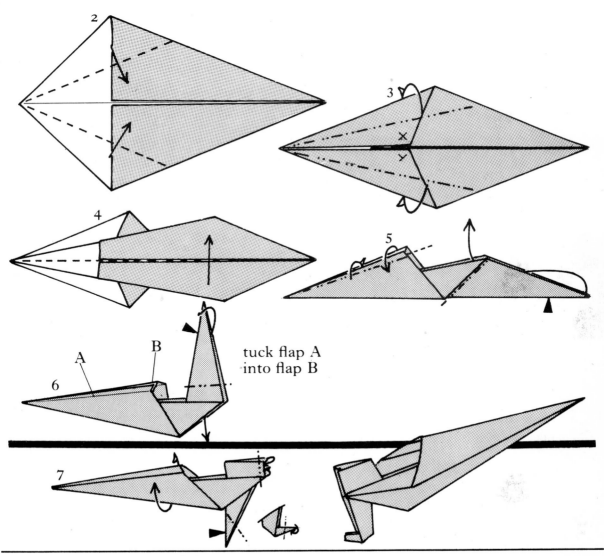

tuck flap A into flap B

(Above) Speedboats
(Left) The Film Star – and a
selection of coloured origami papers
(Opposite) Yachts

Simple Dart John Smith Gt. Britain

An exercise in folding – mostly valley folds.

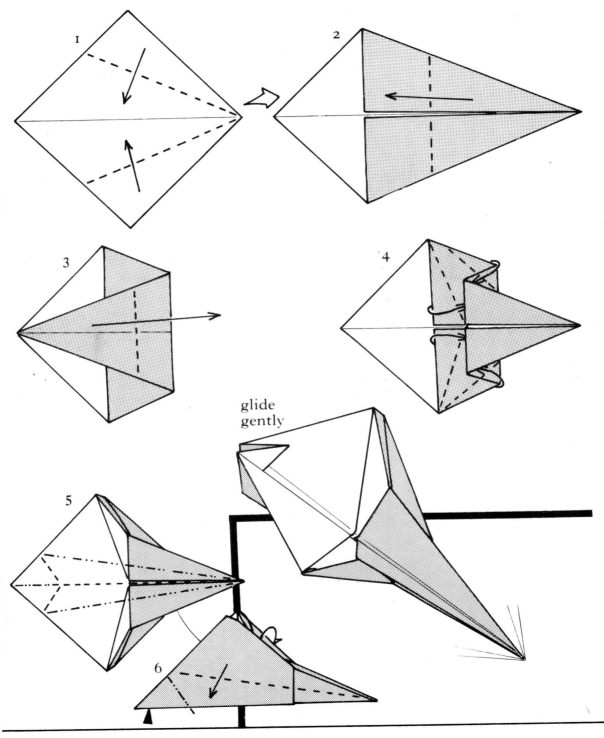

glide
gently

Lakotoi *(New Guinea)* Philip Noble Scotland

Use a square of very thin white paper for this authentic model

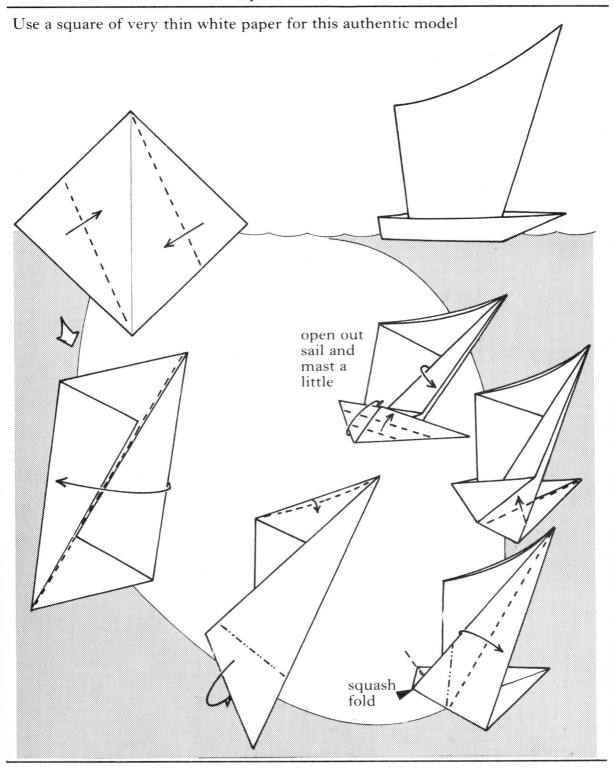

open out
sail and
mast a
little

squash
fold

'No Walk Today' Philip Noble Scotland

Use a square of paper, brown
on one side. Fold in half.
Varied adjustments of the second fold
produce different dogs and pups.

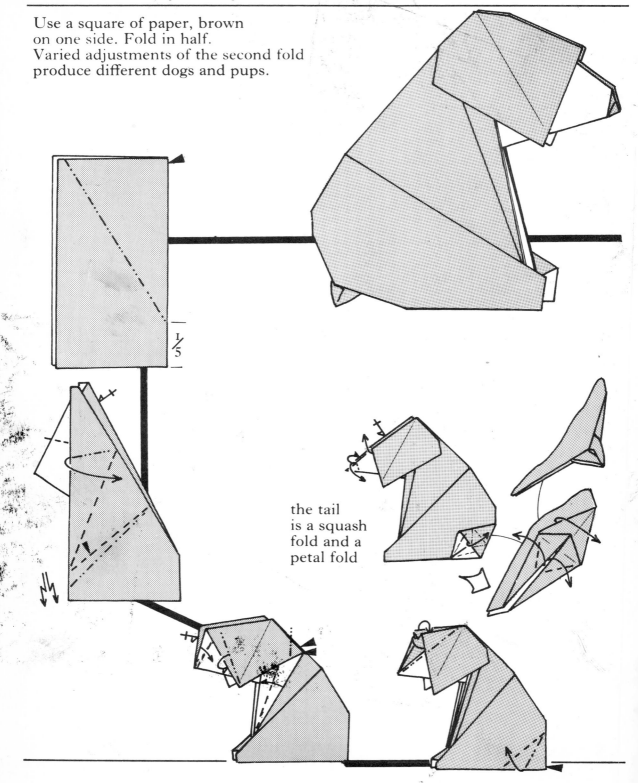

$\frac{1}{5}$

the tail
is a squash
fold and a
petal fold

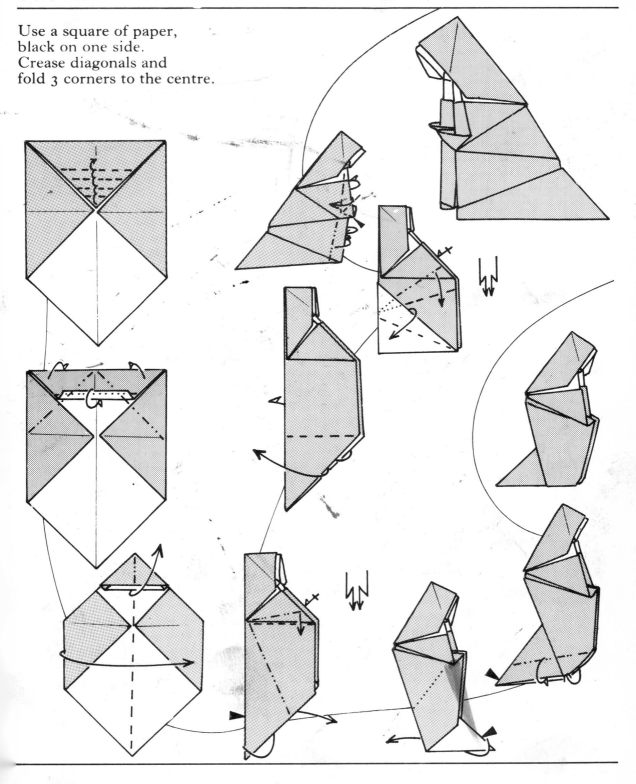

Two Nuns Robert Harbin Gt. Britain

Use a square of paper,
black on one side.
Crease diagonals and
fold 3 corners to the centre.

The Film Star Eric Kenneway Gt. Britain

Use a square of paper, yellow on one side.
Make centre creases as a guide.

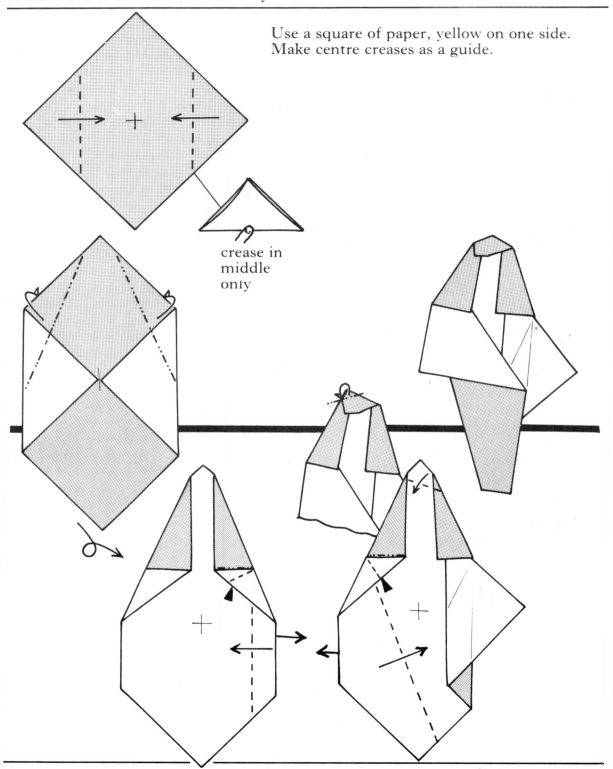

crease in
middle
only

Octahedron (Geometric solid) Patricia Crawford America

Use a square of paper
Crease the diagonals,
fold in half, then fold
points right then left.

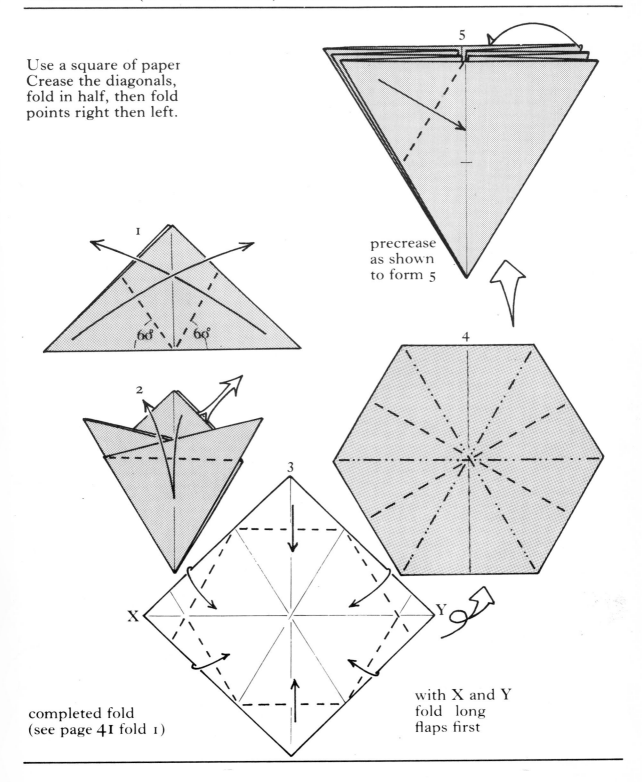

precrease
as shown
to form 5

completed fold
(see page 41 fold 1)

with X and Y
fold long
flaps first

Octahedron *(continued)*

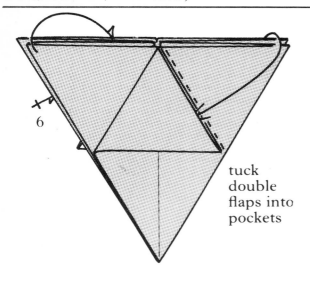

6

tuck
double
flaps into
pockets

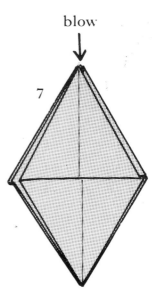

blow

7

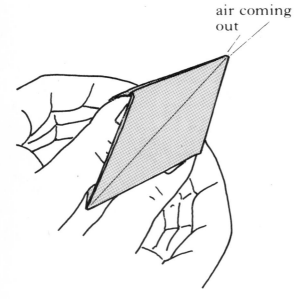

air coming
out

put thumbs
into pockets
to make bellows

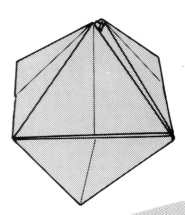

Stalking Cat Patricia Crawford America

Use a square of foil white side down.
Crease diagonals and fold corners as indicated.

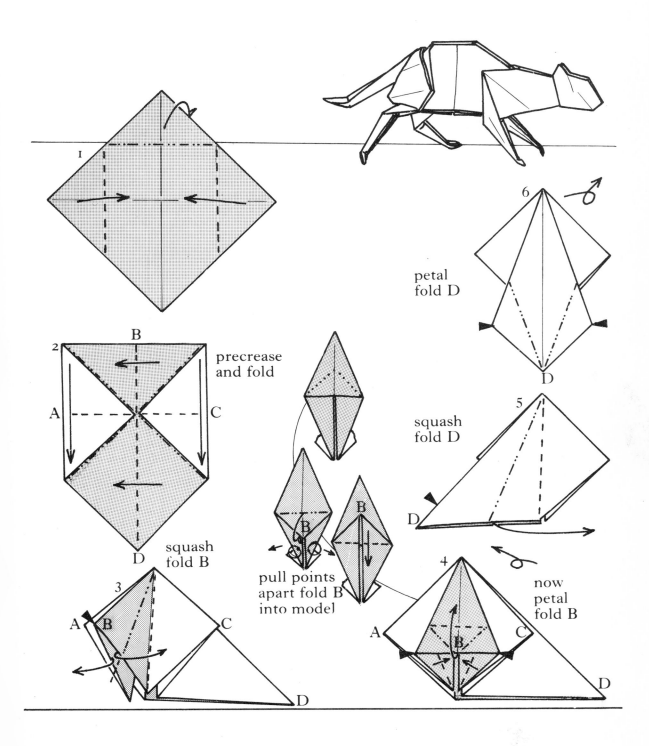

I

B

2

A   C

precrease
and fold

D

squash
fold B

3

A B   C

D

pull points
apart fold B
into model

B

B

4

A   B   C

now
petal
fold B

D

5

squash
fold D

D

6

petal
fold D

D

Stalking Cat *(continued)* *Just concentrate . . .*

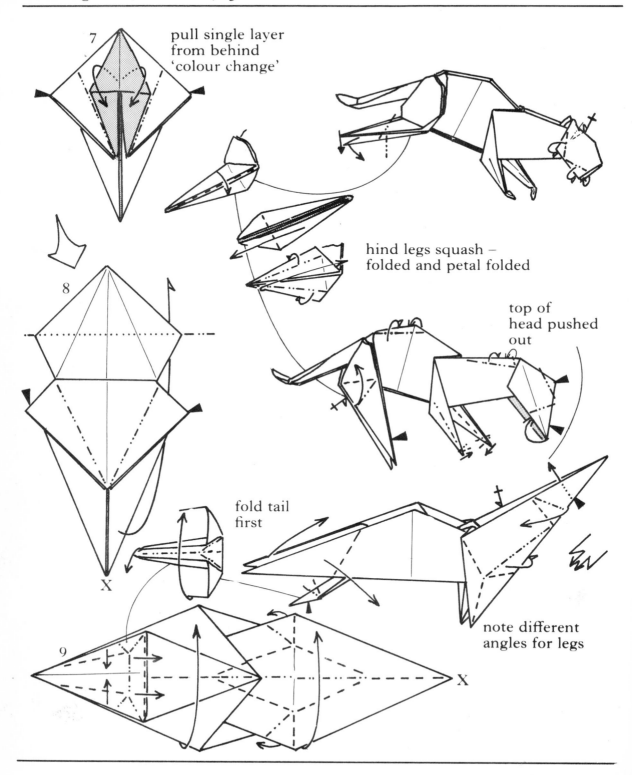

7   pull single layer from behind 'colour change'

hind legs squash – folded and petal folded

top of head pushed out

8

fold tail first

note different angles for legs

X

9

X

Bird Bath Patricia Crawford America

Use a coloured square of foil (6in. × 6in. or 15cm. × 15cm.). Begin
with folds 1, 2 and 3 (page 37) colour side inwards.
Unfold two corners and precrease exactly as indicated.

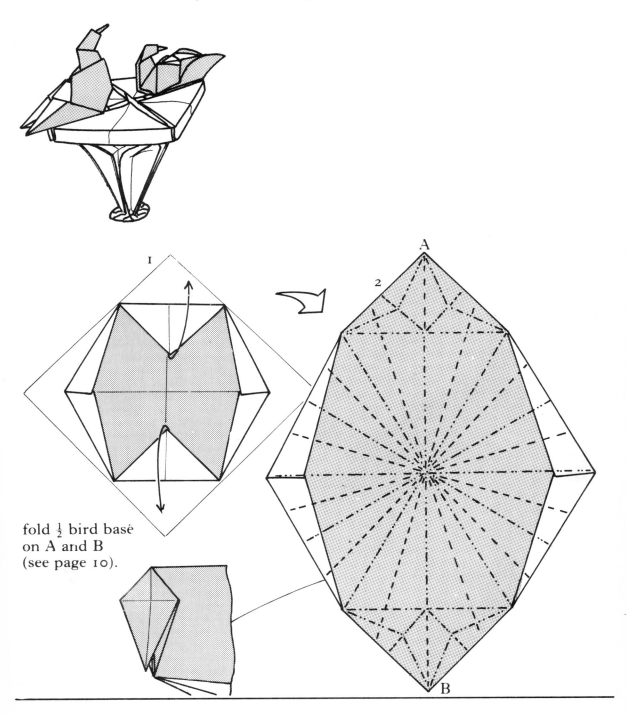

fold ½ bird base
on A and B
(see page 10).

Bird Bath *(continued)*

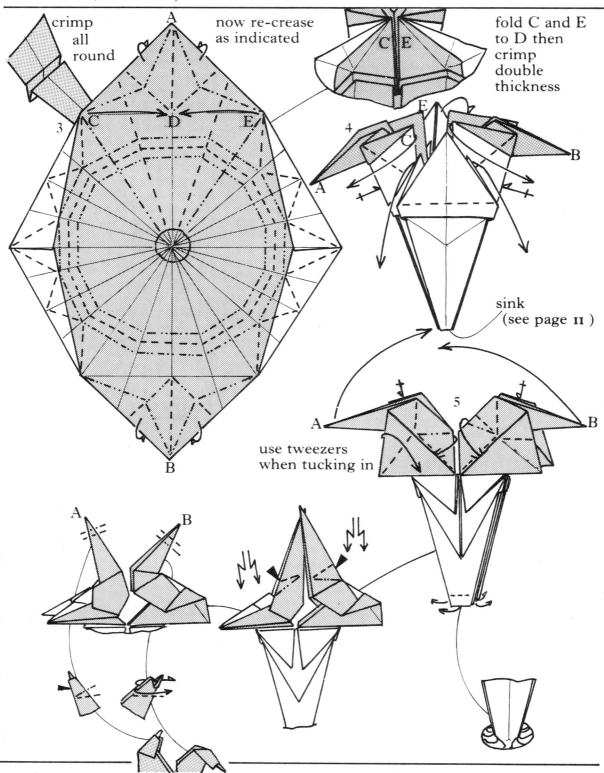

crimp
all
round

A

now re-crease
as indicated

fold C and E
to D then
crimp
double
thickness

C E

3

C   D   E

B

E

4

C

A

B

sink
(see page 11)

A

5

B

use tweezers
when tucking in

A

B

Bird Bath (continued)

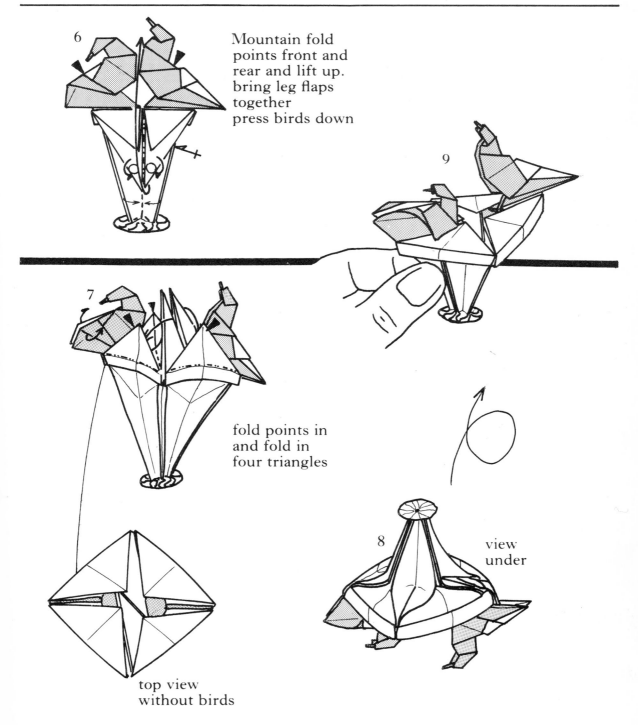

6 Mountain fold points front and rear and lift up. bring leg flaps together press birds down

9

7 fold points in and fold in four triangles

top view without birds

8 view under

Squirrel on a Log Patricia Crawford America

Use a square of foil, gold
or log-like on one side

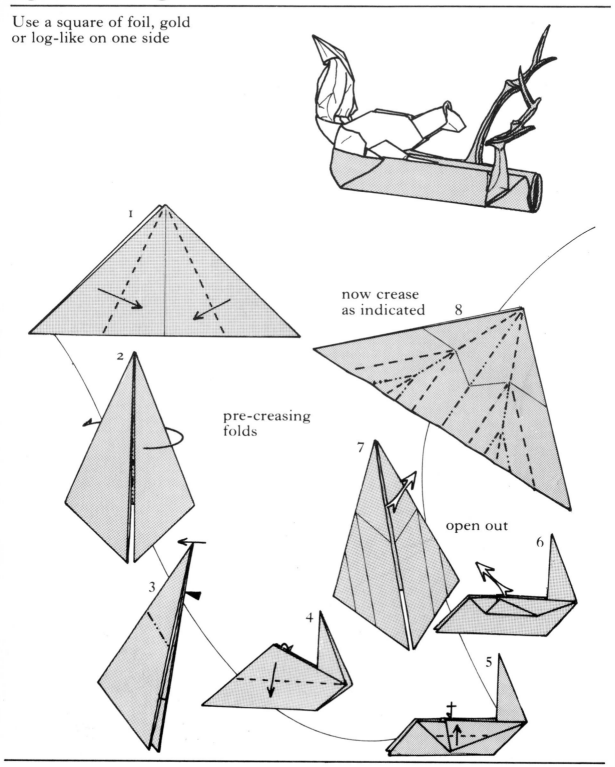

1

2

pre-creasing
folds

3

4

5

6

7

open out

8

now crease
as indicated

Squirrel on a Log *(continued)*

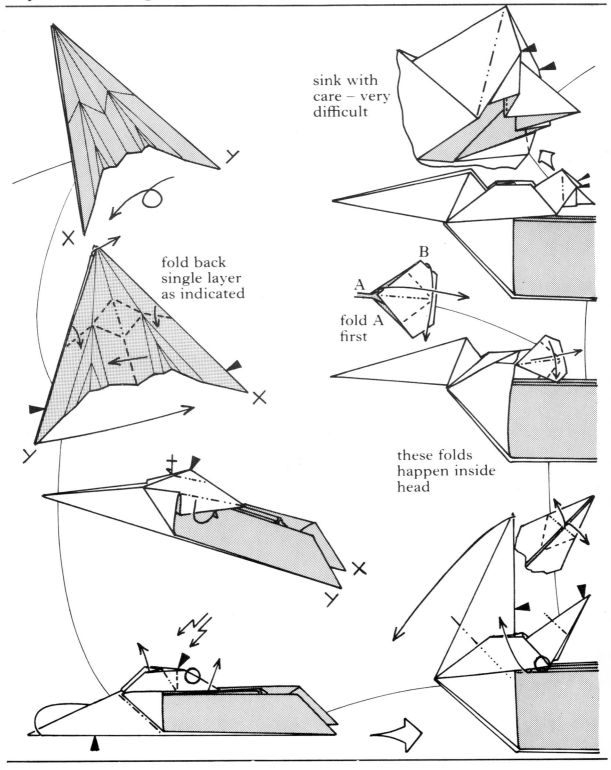

sink with
care – very
difficult

fold back
single layer
as indicated

B

A

fold A
first

these folds
happen inside
head

Squirrel on a Log *(continued)* . . . *watch the sink symbols*

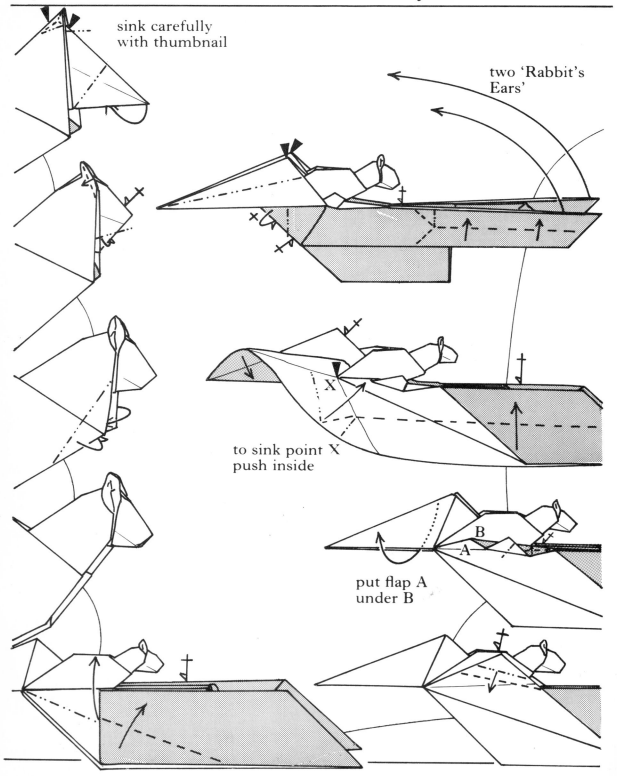

sink carefully
with thumbnail

two 'Rabbit's
Ears'

to sink point X
push inside

put flap A
under B

Squirrel on a Log (continued)

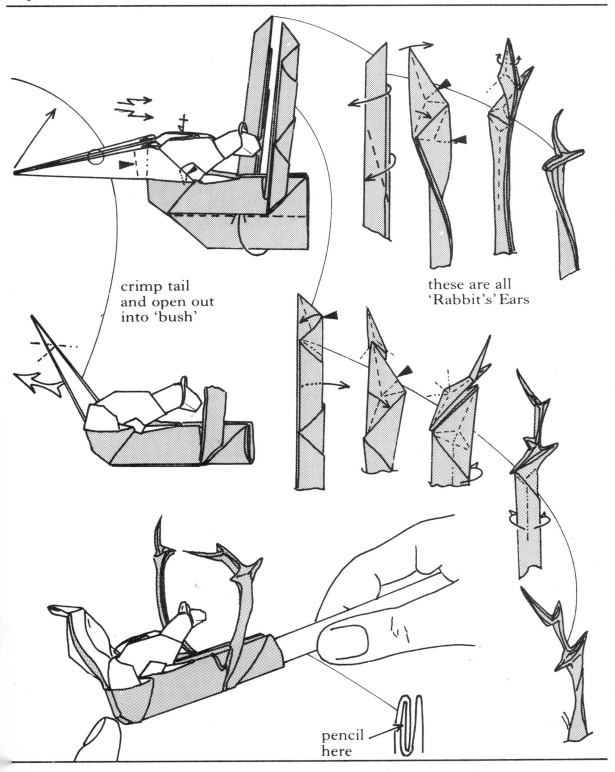

crimp tail
and open out
into 'bush'

these are all
'Rabbit's' Ears

pencil
here

Birds in a Nest Patricia Crawford America

2 × 3 rectangle brown, gold or nestlike on one side.
Foil works well here. Fold very accurately for the best
results.

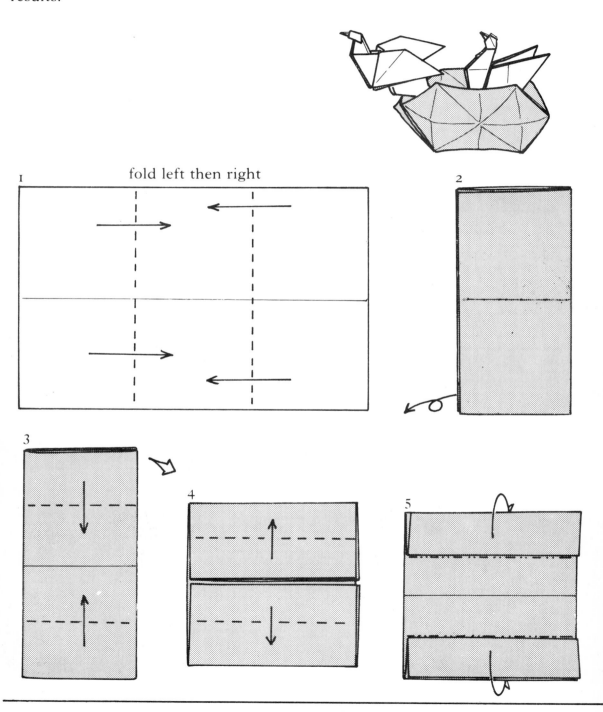

fold left then right

Birds in a Nest *(continued)* . . . *firm creases, please*

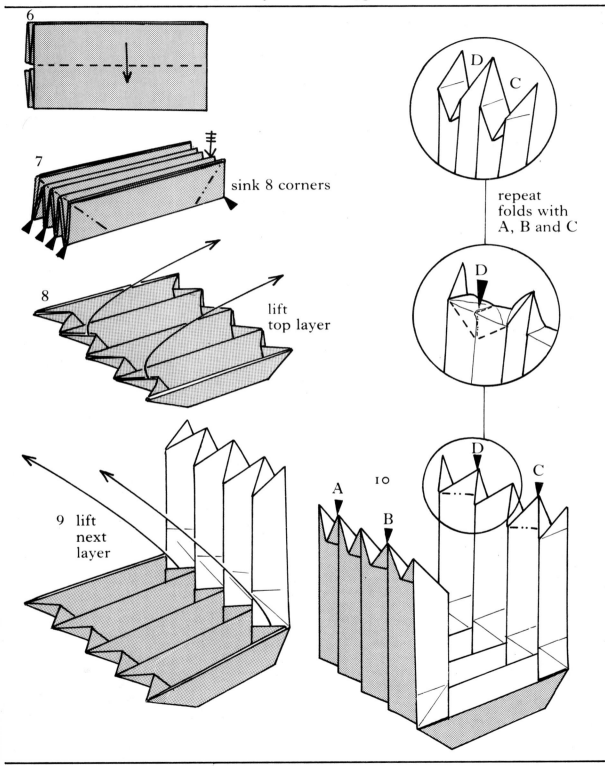

6

7 sink 8 corners

8 lift top layer

9 lift next layer

10

repeat folds with A, B and C

D C

D

D C

A B

(Right) 'No Walk Today'
(Below) The Nun
(Opposite top) Stalking cat
(Opposite below) Bird bath

Birds in a Nest (continued)

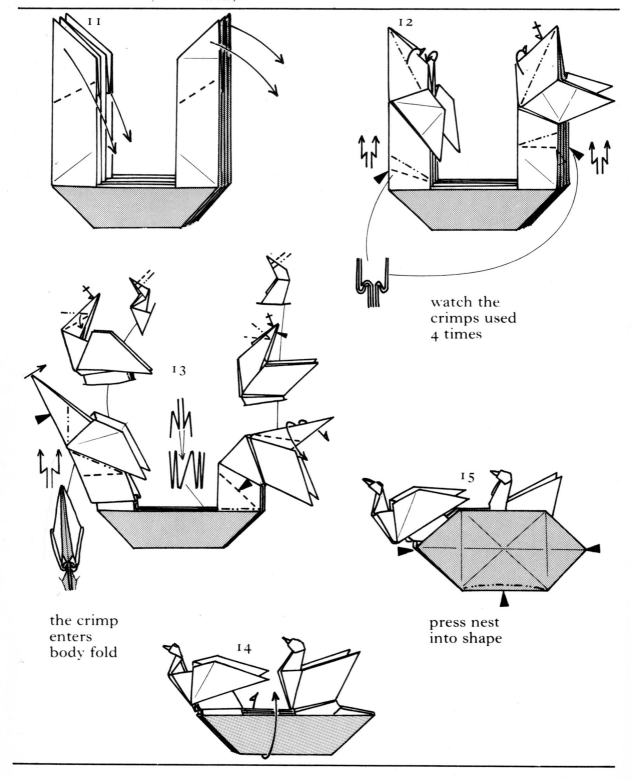

11

12

watch the
crimps used
4 times

13

the crimp
enters
body fold

14

15

press nest
into shape

Mermaid Patricia Crawford America

A square of foil, seaweed green on one side.
Similar preparation to squirrel fold.

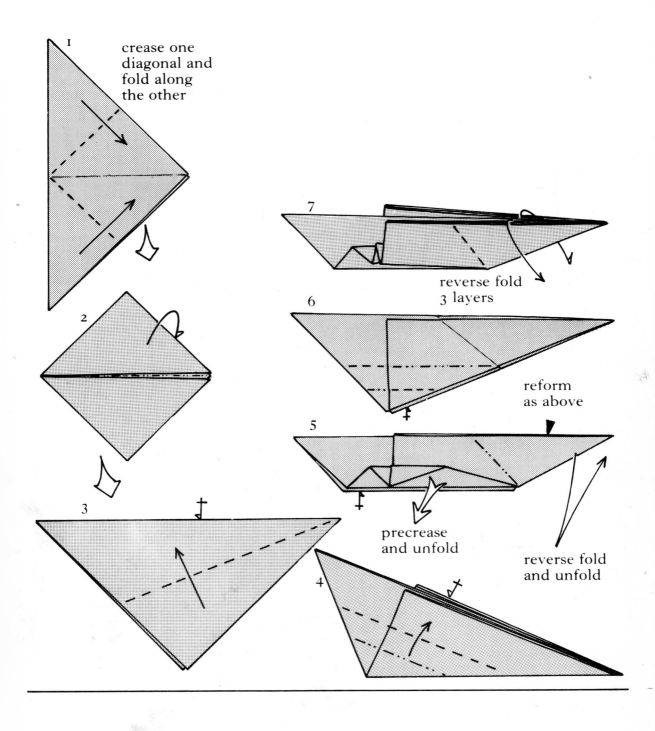

I crease one diagonal and fold along the other

7 reverse fold 3 layers

6 reform as above

5 precrease and unfold reverse fold and unfold

4

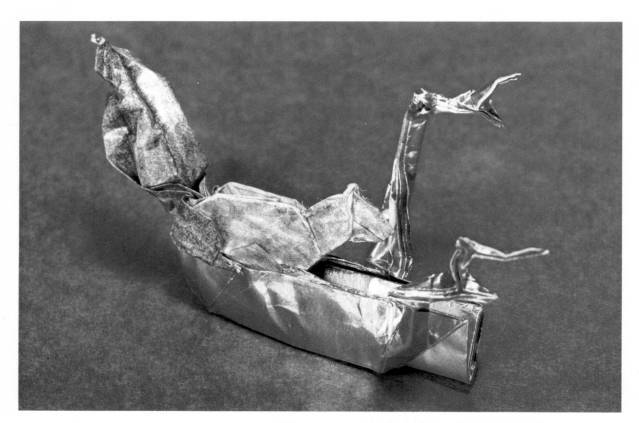

(Above) Squirrel on a log
(Right) Birds in a nest
(Opposite top) Christ on the
Mount of Olives
(Opposite below) The Mermaid

Mermaid *(continued)* ... *very difficult folds ahead*

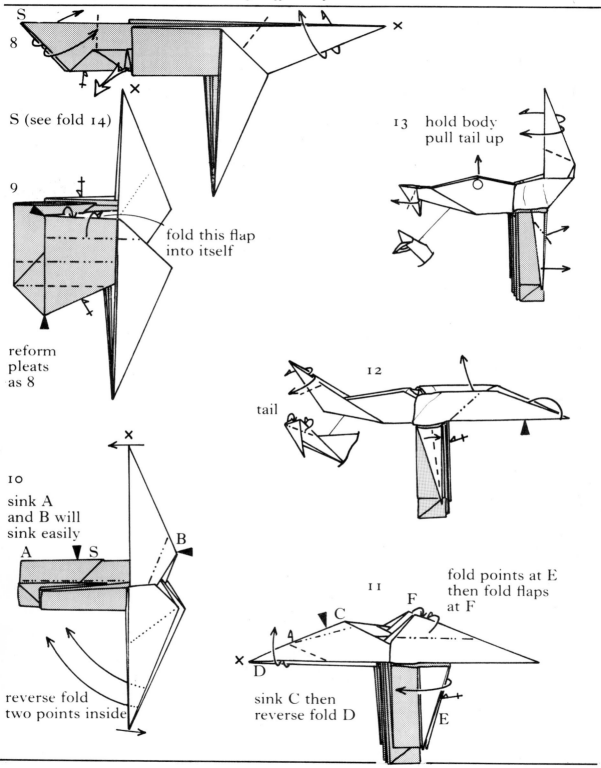

S

8

S (see fold 14)

9

fold this flap into itself

reform
pleats
as 8

13 hold body
pull tail up

12

tail

10

sink A
and B will
sink easily

A ▼ S   B ▼

reverse fold
two points inside

11   F

fold points at E
then fold flaps
at F

▼ C

D

sink C then
reverse fold D

E

Mermaid *(continued)*

pull out S see
folds 8, 9 and 10

round the body
by squeezing and
open out seaweed
as indicated

The Swan

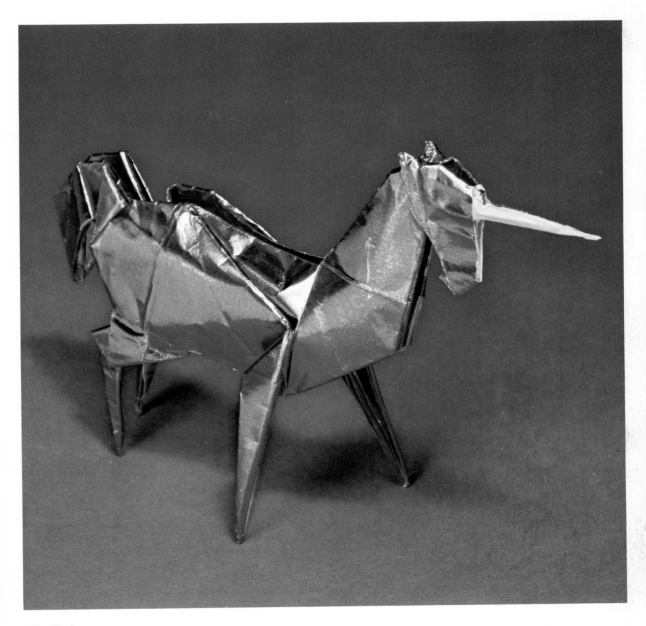

The Unicorn

Christ on the Mount of Olives Patricia Crawford America

Use a square of foil
Begin fold 8 of the Mermaid (page 56)
Note slight alteration in 1

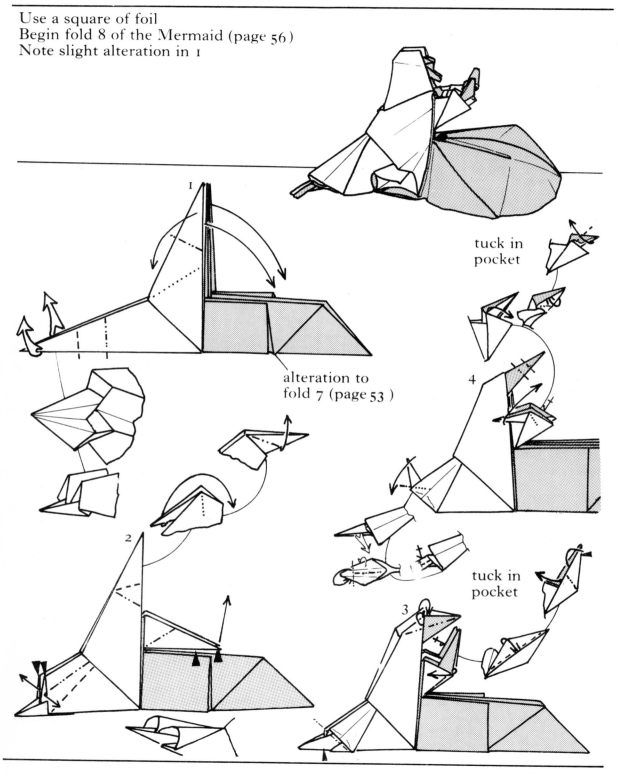

tuck in
pocket

alteration to
fold 7 (page 53)

4

tuck in
pocket

2

3

Christ on the Mount of Olives *(continued)*

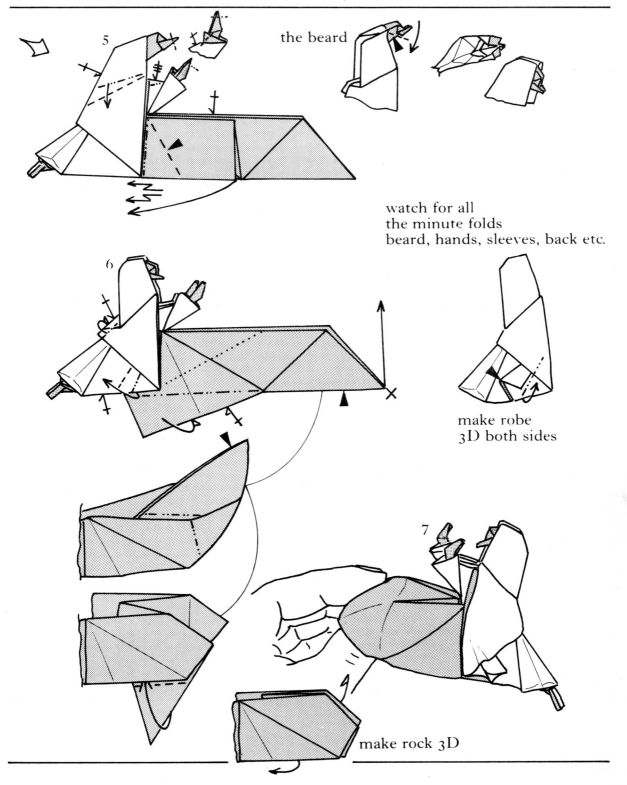

5

the beard

watch for all
the minute folds
beard, hands, sleeves, back etc.

6

make robe
3D both sides

7

make rock 3D

Kangaroo

(Above) Scorpion
(Left) Square-rigged ship

Swan Patricia Crawford America

Begin with a BIRD BASE
(page 10 fold 20).
Stretch the base
both ways to precrease
large thin white square

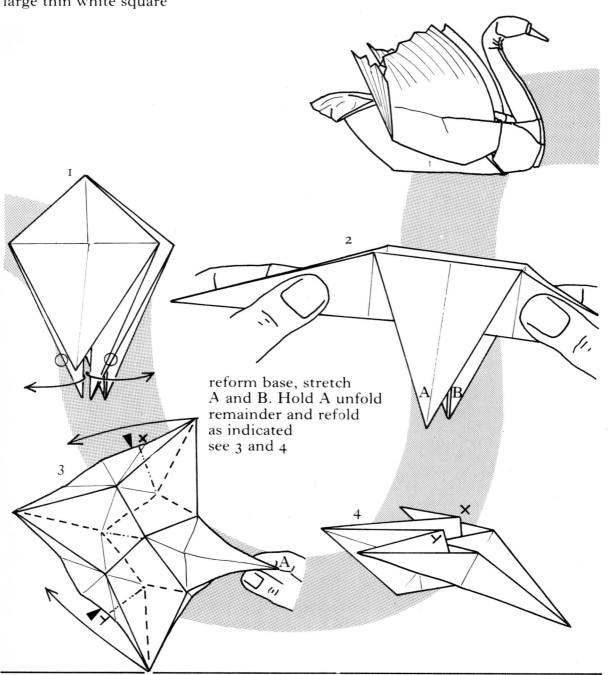

reform base, stretch
A and B. Hold A unfold
remainder and refold
as indicated
see 3 and 4

Swan (continued)

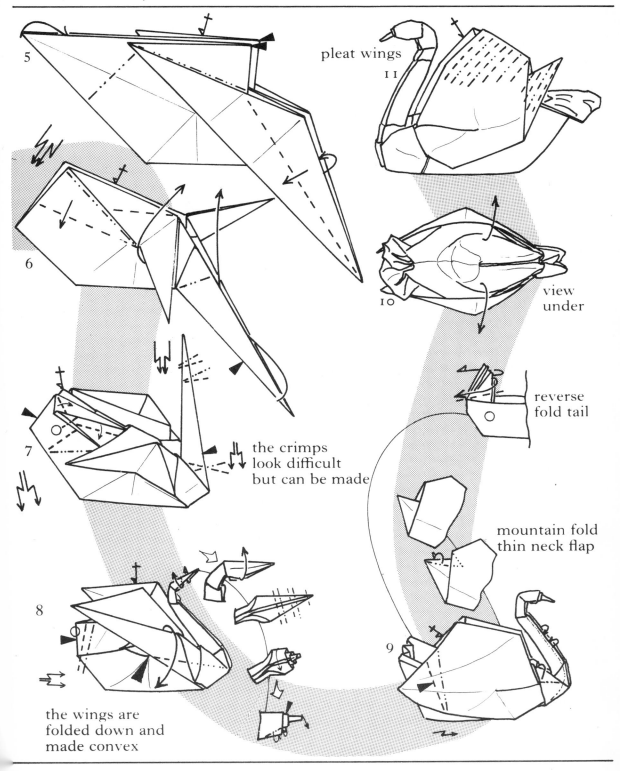

5

6

pleat wings
11

10

view under

7

the crimps look difficult but can be made

reverse fold tail

mountain fold thin neck flap

8

9

the wings are folded down and made convex

Unicorn Patricia Crawford America

Use a square of foil. Begin with
fold 2 of the Mermaid (page 53)

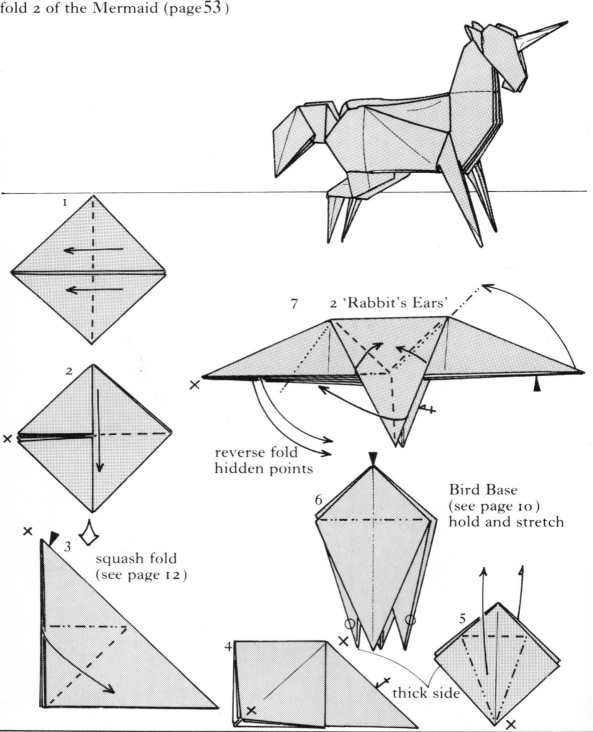

1

7   2 'Rabbit's Ears'

2

reverse fold
hidden points

Bird Base
(see page 10)
hold and stretch

6

squash fold
(see page 12)

3

5

4

thick side

Unicorn (continued)

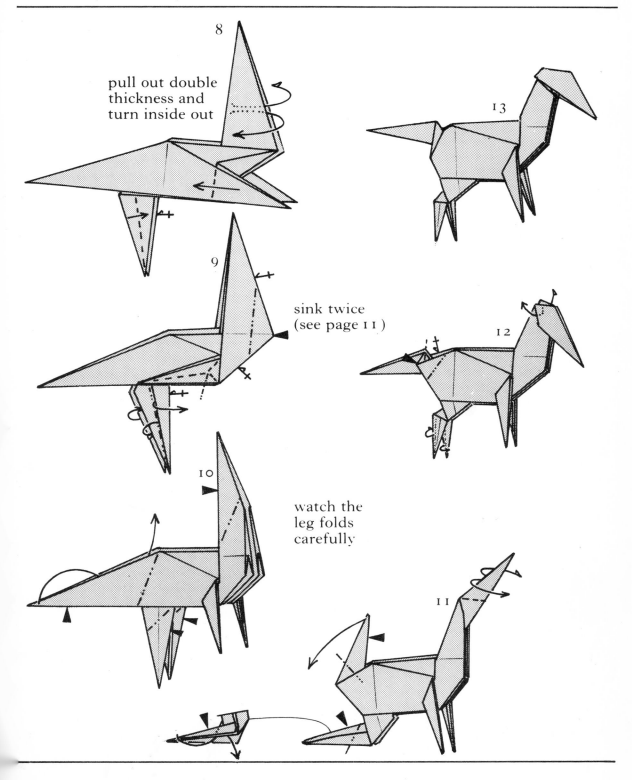

8

pull out double
thickness and
turn inside out

13

9

sink twice
(see page 11)

12

10

watch the
leg folds
carefully

11

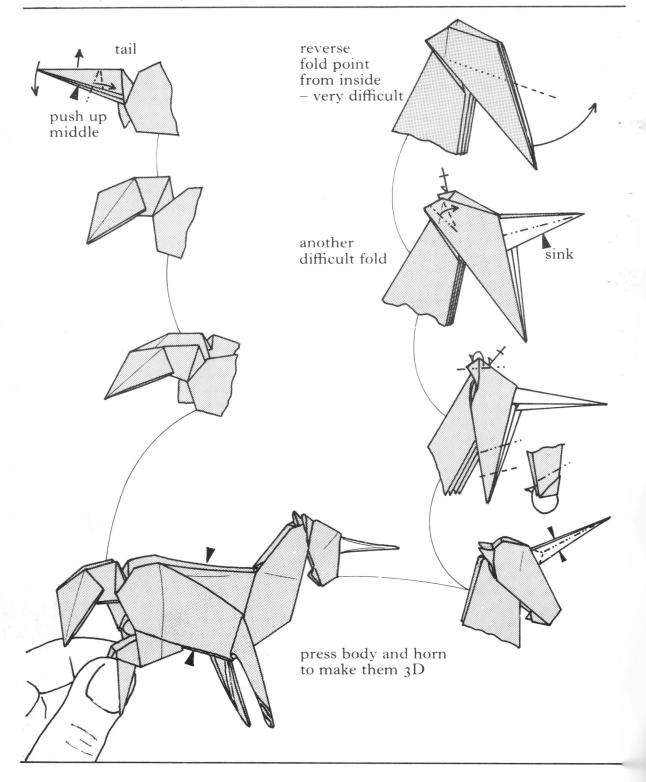

tail

push up
middle

reverse
fold point
from inside
– very difficult

another
difficult fold

sink

press body and horn
to make them 3D

Kangaroo Patricia Crawford America

Crease a square in the centre only and valley fold 3 corners.
Then turn over and carefully precrease as indicated.

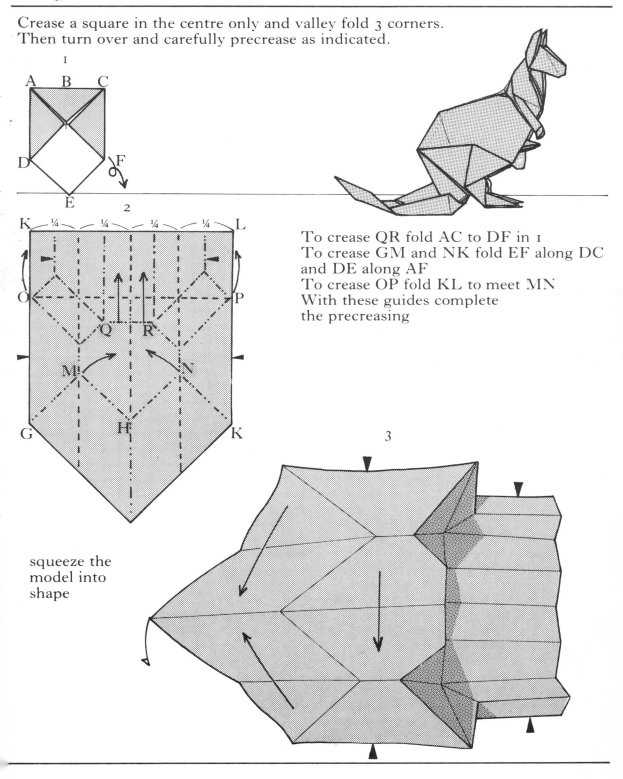

To crease QR fold AC to DF in 1
To crease GM and NK fold EF along DC
and DE along AF
To crease OP fold KL to meet MN
With these guides complete
the precreasing

squeeze the
model into
shape

Kangaroo *(continued)*

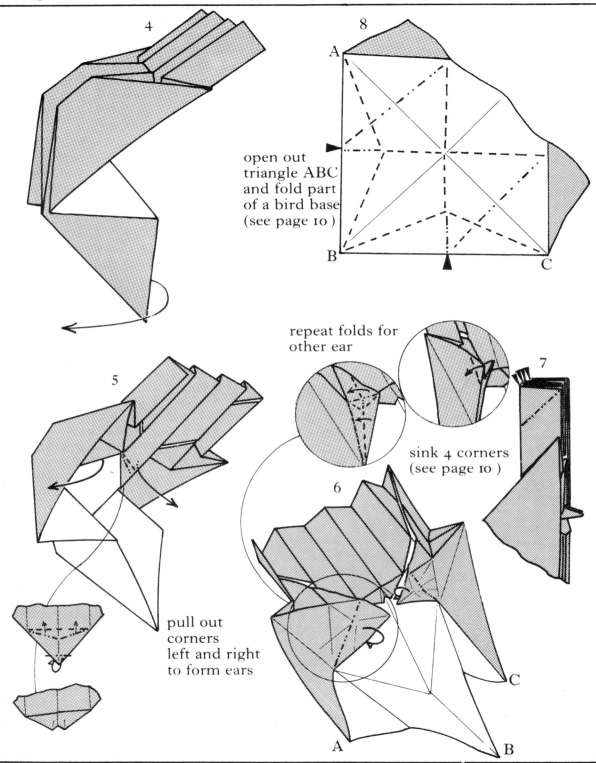

4

8

A

open out
triangle ABC
and fold part
of a bird base
(see page 10)

B   C

5

repeat folds for
other ear

7

sink 4 corners
(see page 10)

6

pull out
corners
left and right
to form ears

A   B

C

Kangaroo *(continued)*

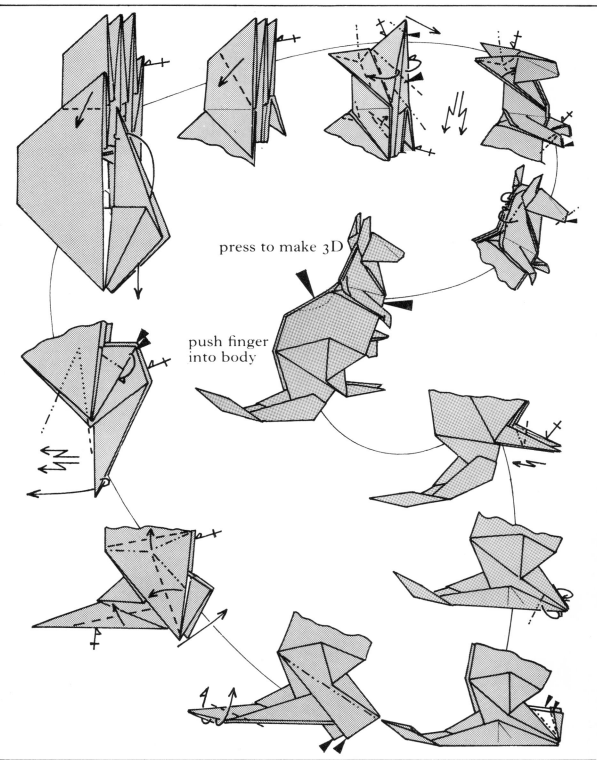

press to make 3D

push finger
into body

Scorpion Patricia Crawford America

Use a dark green square of foil.
Begin with a PRELIMINARY BASE.
(see page 9 fold 9)

1

squash 4 corners
form frog base

6

2

petal fold

3

5

push sides in

4

Scorpion *(continued)*

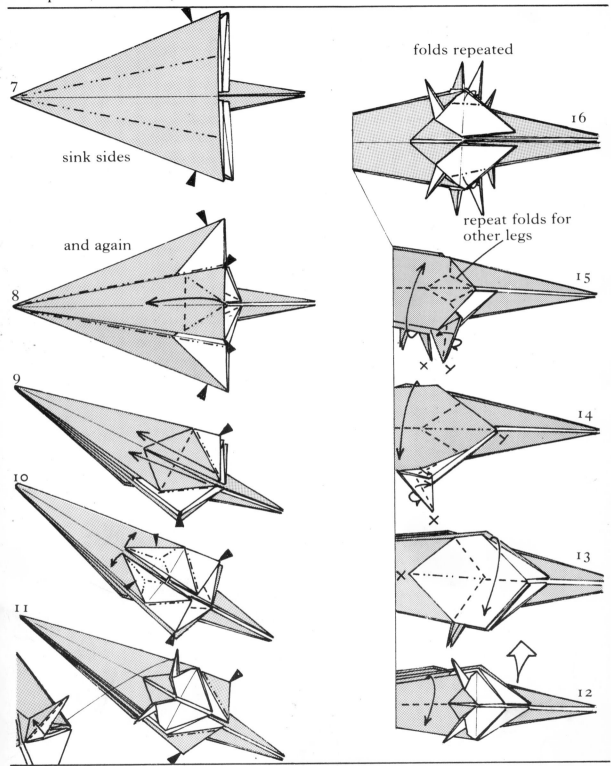

7

sink sides

and again

8

9

10

11

folds repeated

16

repeat folds for
other legs

15

14

13

12

Scorpion *(continued)*

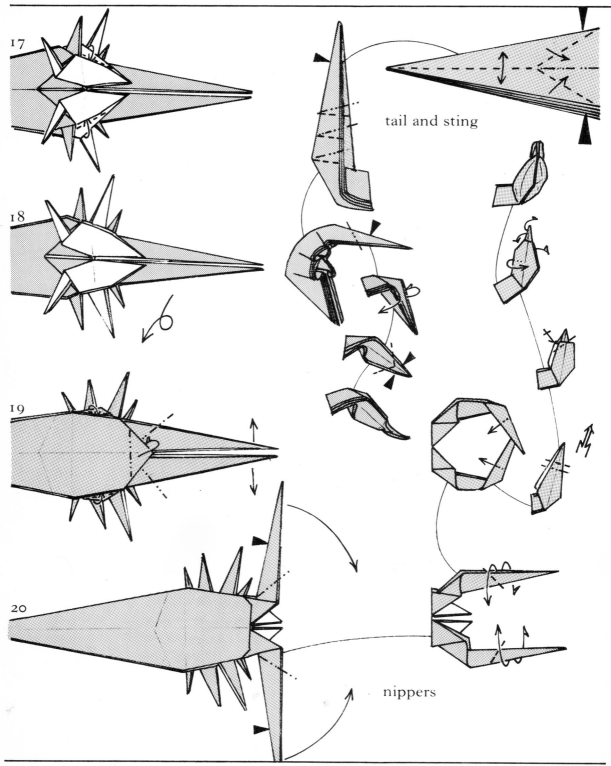

17

18

19

20

tail and sting

nippers

Full-rigged Ship Patricia Crawford America

Use a square of red foil.
Begin with a BIRD BASE (see page 10)

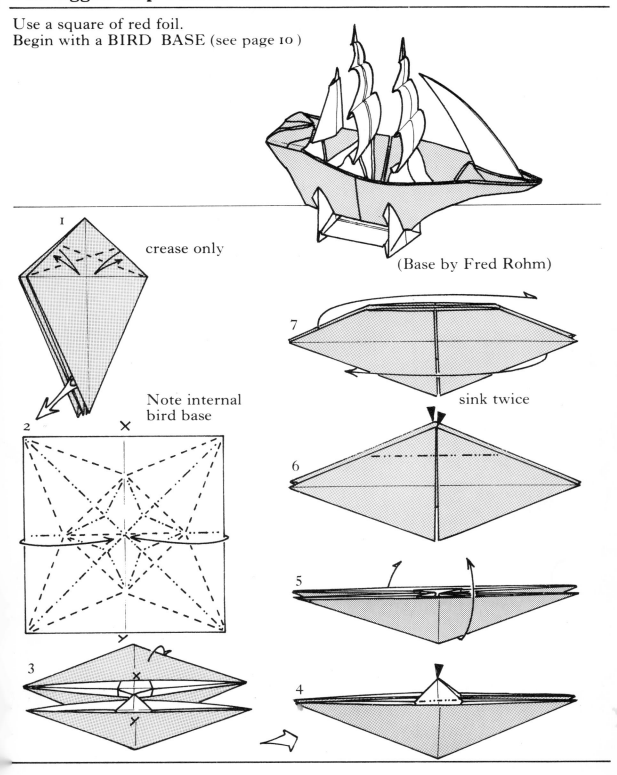

crease only

(Base by Fred Rohm)

Note internal
bird base

sink twice

Full-rigged Ship *(continued)*

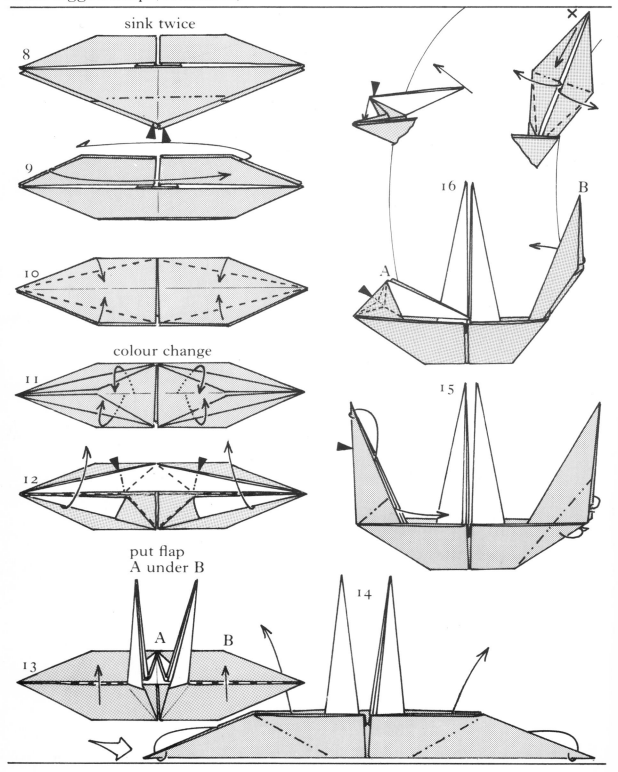

sink twice

8

9

10

colour change

11

12

put flap
A under B

A B

13

14

15

16

A

B

Full-rigged Ship *(continued)*

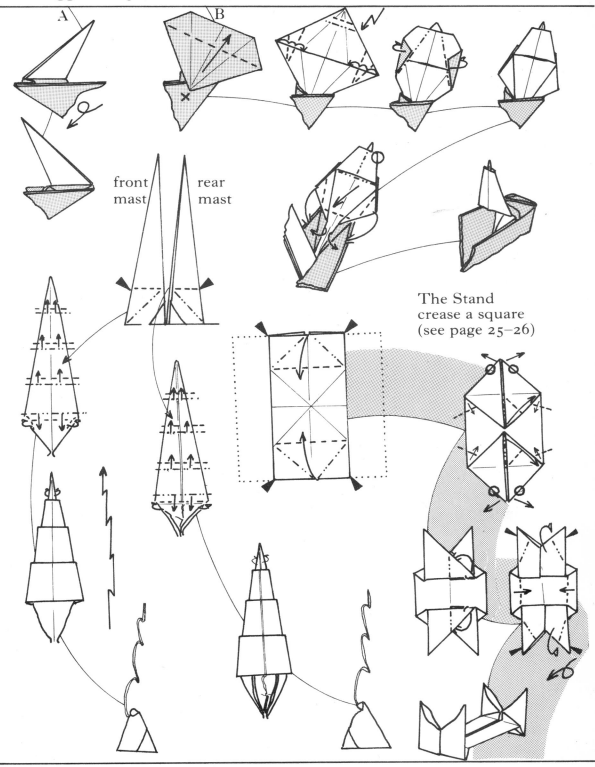

A B

front mast   rear mast

The Stand
crease a square
(see page 25–26)

Bibliography

Here is a list of a few books on Origami which are fairly easy to find:—

Harbin, Robert *Paper Magic*, John Maxfield Ltd. *Origami 1, 2* and *3*, Hodder Paperbacks, Funk and Wagnalls, New York. *Secrets of Origami*, Oldbourne, London, Book Sales, America.

Kasahara, Kunihilo *Creative Origami*, a luxury book obtainable in larger book shops.

Kenneway, Eric *Simple Origami, Origami in Action*, both contain fine models published by the Dryad Press, Leicester.

Lewis, Shari and Openheimer *Folding Paper Puppets. Folding Paper Toys*. Stein and Day, New York.

Nakano, Dokouhtei Correspondence course of Origami, Nakano Origami Institute, 32/6 Kamikitazawa 3-Chome, Setagaya-Ku Tokyo, 156 Japan. Write for particulars.

Randlett, Samuel *The Art of Origami* and *The Best of Origami*, E. P. Dutton and Co. Inc., New York. Faber and Faber, London. Outstanding material.

Takahama, Toshie *Creative Life with Creative Origami*, obtainable from:— The Origami Center, 71 West 11th Street, New York, 2NY USA.

Suppliers of Origami paper and books:—
U.S.A.
The Origami Center, 71 West 11th Street, New York. 2NY USA.
Great Britain
John Maxfield, 9 The Broadway, Mill Hill, London NW7.